PRAISE FOR EVENING ECHOES

Tracy Alan Barnett has a way of finding the profound meaning in the simple moments of life. His first book, **Whispers in the Morning**, helped readers to experience the tenor and tone of God's voice. His present offering, **Evening Echoes,** reminds readers that God continues to speak in a still small voice in times of uncertainty. Tracy Barnett is a loving husband, doting father, trusted friend and amazing gift to the body of Christ. We are blessed to have such a fresh sound among us.

Michael Steve Brown, Pastor
True Vision Church
San Antonio, Texas

In times of divisiveness and acrimony in almost every place, even the church, there needs to be a voice that has the Heart of a Pastor (the Church) and the Soul of a Chaplain (the World) to remind us that in each and every moment of life, God is Present, God Cares, and God has a Purpose for our lives, even in the most difficult and demanding times of our lives. Chaplain, Pastor, and Teacher Tracy Barnett is that voice. I have already been blessed immensely to know the man himself and his gentle, yet powerful voice of compassion, comfort, and challenge. I would invite anyone in need of a 'Word' from the Lord to pick up this book and find yourself at the feet of the Master Jesus and one of His disciples, Chaplain Tray Barnett.

James Duke, Rev. Dr. Chaplain
ACPE Educator
Houston, TX

I am delighted to write any word on behalf of my friend and brother, Tracy (Tray) Barnett. The hand of the Lord is on him in a remarkable way. Tracy is a walking example of life stories. I am convinced the Lord has raised up a fresh voice and given him an unusual ability to take his life stories and link them to the word of God and share them in a visual encouraging way. I have been blessed by this book and I have no doubt this book will be a blessing to you. I am sure you will want to recommend it to all your friends.

James Chester, Rev. Dr., Senior Pastor
Orthodox Zion
West Palm Beach, Florida

Not many things make it to my nightstand: my cell phone, my glasses and now *Evening Echoes*. There are times when life becomes complicated with its twists and turns, but in those uncertain times, Evening Echoes provides a means through which you can: find peace of mind; be reminded that you can make it; know that it's not over until God says it's over; be persuaded that you have a safe place; experience mercy that's new every morning; rely on the promises of God; be inspired that there is always hope; and call to mind that compassion is always in order. ***Evening Echoes*** emerges from the heart of the author, Tracy Alan Barnett, and speaks from personal experiences to which we can all relate. I especially recall The Fern, "It just needs rain, and it comes back to life." ***Evening Echoes*** is a great read for anytime and conveys God's possibilities for your life.

Pastor Barbara L Taylor
New Vision Full Gospel Ministry
Philadelphia, PA

Tracy Alan Barnett, a brother and humble scholar, has encouraged me personally and those of our ministry here at the New Bethel Missionary Baptist Church, West Palm Beach Florida through his first book, ***"Whispers in the Morning."*** I'm excited about his work he now shares in ***"Evening Echoes,"*** a perfect formula for family devotions, ministry meetings, preaching illustrations and so much more. Blessings to you my friend.

Toby Philpart, Senior Pastor
New Bethel Missionary Baptist Church
West Palm Beach Florida

He's done it again! Tracy Alan Barnett has a way of writing that pulls the reader into real life stories, and then gently lands them in the hands of helpful and encouraging scripture passages that speak to the heart of the matter. I'm particularly fond of day three entitled, "Call

Me," when he honors the calls of his son's voice, recalling the times when God hears us. Barnett is insightful, funny and smart, and talks about real life application. I highly recommend "*Evening Echoes.*"

Russell Howelton, Pastor
Skybridge Community Church
San Antonio, TX

EVENING
Echoes

A Guide to Discovering God's Voice in the Quiet Moments

TRACY ALAN BARNETT

ISBN: 978-1-7338851-2-6

Library of Congress Control Number: 2020904983

Printed in San Antonio, TX by Tracy Alan Barnett

Photo for Author page by Patrick Dean of Images by Patrick

While all attempts have been made to verify information provided for this publication, the author and publisher assume no responsibility for errors, omissions, or contrary interpretation of the subject matter herein.

For bulk book orders, contact Tracy Alan Barnett, using email address WhsprsMorn@gmail.com.

Dedication

To my wife, Carla, who is brilliant, beautiful, and the greatest blessing in my life.

To my sons Branden and Bryson, all my nieces and nephews. I love each of you and I am excited to see what the future holds for you. I pray this book encourages you to trust God, dream big dreams, and dedicate yourself to making those dreams become a reality.

In the memory of two men who have forever impacted my life and made me a better man: my father, Alvin Barnett, Sr. and my father-in-law, Karia McMillon. I am eternally grateful for your encouragement and support.

Finally, to all the servicemen and women with whom I 've had the honor of serving alongside. God bless you.

TABLE OF CONTENTS

INTRODUCTION

West Palm Beach, Florida
2/28/2019 7:00 PM

The voice on the other end of the phone shattered the peace of a quiet evening, "How soon can you make it back to the hospital? We've got a report of an active shooter in the hospital, and they're asking for the Chaplains to respond." I could hear myself saying, "I'm on my way," before I could even analyze what was said. I stared at the silent cellphone for a moment, and then a hundred questions popped into my mind. He'd said, "active shooter." Did that mean the shooter was still in the hospital roaming the hallways, terrorizing people? Were there casualties? How many people were hurt? There was no way this situation could be good, I mean, they were calling for the Chaplains. That couldn't be a good sign.

As I murmur to myself, I find that I sound like all of the people I've watched on TV over the years. *How could this happen here?* I would have never thought something like this would happen at this hospital. *What is wrong with people?* Well, I guess I can't be too surprised. Evil tends to pop up where we least expect it. As I speed toward the hospital, I realize I hadn't spoken to my wife, and this might make the news, so I send her a quick text message (*Hey, called back to the hospital for an emergency. Report of an active shooter. I'm fine. TTYL*). I send another group text to family members, so they know I'm okay, and my phone doesn't get overrun with phone calls of concern asking if I'm okay. As I speed toward the hospital, I whisper a prayer.

I pray for those that might be injured. I pray for the families affected. I pray for those treating the wounded. I pray for the shooter. I pray for the responders and officers I greet every morning. I pray that God gives me strength for whatever I am about to encounter and quiet my spirit to use me to minister to the hurt, confused, and those stunned into disbelief. I pray that God will use me through the Ministry of Presence. Winnifred Fallers Sullivan defined the Ministry of Presence as, "a form of servanthood characterized by suffering alongside the hurt and oppressed."

Lord, prepare me to suffer alongside those hurting right now.

I can see the flashing red and blue lights of police vehicles as I turn the corner. As I drive down the driveway, the bank of lights from the local news stations pierces the cover of night, turning the evening into an eerie artificial day. I make a quick stop to my office to retrieve my hat that reads, 'Chaplain,' so people know who I am without having to ask. I start walking toward the scene of the incident, and ready myself again for what may be around the corner. I feel my heart race a little as I walk past the suspicious gaze of the FBI agents. A security guard's voice, who must have noticed my hat and my credentials hanging around my neck, catches my attention as he says, "Hey, Chaplain, everyone is down that way. They're waiting for you." He points toward the hallway leading to the emergency room, and as he points, in my mind, I remember a moment when I was sitting in Saudi Arabia in 1998 at the Prince Sultan Air Base.

I was the Superintendent of the 1621st Air Mobility Squadron Command Post deployed in support of Operation Southern Watch. On August 7, 1998, the Command Post received

notification of an attack on two US Embassies
in Africa. The US Embassy in Dar es Salaam,
Tanzania, and the embassy in Nairobi, Kenya,
were simultaneously attacked with a coor-
dinated suicide truck bomb. A little-known
group named Al-Qaeda and its little-known
leader named Osama Bin-Laden announced
an open war on the United States by attacking
the embassies. The attack injured more than
4000 and killed 224 people. The Prince Sultan
Air Base led the humanitarian response, and
the command post played a central role in
coordinating the effort. I had an office located
near the runway, and after helping to respond
to the incident, I walked out of the office and
saw a sea of coffins waiting to be loaded on
the next aircraft and taken to the scene of the
attacks. As I stood at the sea, I realized those
coffins weren't meant for those killed in Africa
but meant to carry me and those serving with
me home, if the enemy had a little better aim.
As I looked over the sea, the fragility of life
consumed me, and the reality hit me that
what the enemy tries to do is steal life away
quickly. Jesus' words came to mind as I stood
at the sea: *"The thief comes only to steal, kill, and
destroy, but I came that they may have life and*

have it abundantly (John 10:10)." A thief had sto-
len innocence lives, but as I stood there, what
echoed inside of me were the words of the one
who said, despite the thief, he had come to
give me abundant life. As I draw closer to the
emergency room, I wonder if I am approach-
ing another sea.

I take a deep breath and do my best to
grab hold of my anxiety. As the Chaplain,
I strive to be the non-anxious presence in a
room filled with anxiety. It is my role in pro-
viding pastoral care to suffer alongside those
who are suffering, and yet represent the one
who can help them in their suffering. I push
open the door, and to my great relief, there
is no sea, but a room full of people shocked,
stunned in disbelief, and others comforting one another. Occasionally, I could see
silent tears falling from eyes, as individuals thought about how they had escaped
death that night. I could hear the outbursts
of sadness and pain, mixed with thoughts
of gratefulness. My role, at this moment, is
to hold their hands, walk with them, comfort them, and echo through my actions, the
words of Jesus said in John 10:10. My very
presence declares that despite what the thief

attempted to steal that night, there is still a promise of abundant life.

In my moments of crisis, I have discovered what God has whispered to me in the morning, echoes through the evening, and sustains me until the breaking of day. My prayer for you as you read this book is that in your crisis or moments of despair, perhaps one of the following devotionals will echo in your evening until you see the breaking of the day. I pray this for you because despite what the thief tries, God still promises us life and life more abundantly.

How to Get the Most Out of This Guide

This devotional guide is designed as a tool and roadmap to help you hear God speaking in your daily life. First, I encourage you to read the devotional and reflect on your life experiences and how you might identify with the devotional. Secondly, I encourage you to open your Bible and read the theme scripture and back story attached to each devotional to understand the context of the scripture. Finally, after reading the devotional and the scripture, take a moment and write a reflection in the space provided at the end of each chapter, so you can consider how God is speaking to you in your current situation.

I pray as you read and spend more time in God's Word, your faith is increased, and your hope restored. It is my deepest desire that this book helps each of you connect to God's purpose and plan for your life.

CHAPTER 1

ECHOES OF ENDURANCE

*"Endurance is not just the ability
to bear hard things,
but to turn it into glory."*

William Barclay

I GOT THE BOOT

*"How lovely is your dwelling place, O LORD
OF HEAVEN'S ARMIES. I LONG, YES, I
FAINT WITH LONGING to enter the courts of
the LORD. With my whole being, body and
soul, I will shout joyfully to the living God."*

Psalm 84: 1-2

My youngest son taught me one of the greatest lessons I ever learned about the difference between being present and having someone's presence. We lived in the DC area years ago, and if you've ever lived in the DMV (District of Columbia, Maryland, and Virginia) area, you understand how traffic can be a challenge. We lived in Virginia, but I worked in Maryland. It was roughly a 25-mile trip, but if I left at the wrong time, it could take an hour or longer to get to work. The trip home was even worse. I found myself leaving home early in the morning and coming home late.

I came home one day, tired and exhausted from the day. My four-year-old son, full of energy and excitement, met me at the door and said, "Come on, Daddy, let's play." I told him in a tone meant to run him off for a few minutes, "Can I just get in the door and take off my boots?" He literally took two steps back and let me walk into the house. What he did next almost brought me to tears. He fell on his knees and began to unlace my boots. I told him, "Whatever you want to do, let's do that." We turned around, walked back outside, and tossed around the football.

The next day I came home, and as my key hit the door, I heard my son running down the stairs, yelling, "I got the boot! I got the boot! I got the boot!" He slid across the floor and began to unlace my boots. I said, "Whatever you want to do, let's do that." The scene repeated itself the next day. He ran, shouting, "I got the boot! I got the boot!"

The following day my older son must have figured something out, because then I heard two sets of voices yelling, "I got the boot! No, I got the boot! I got the boot! No, I got the boot," and two bodies came skidding across the floor, trying to unlace my boots. The excitement of getting in Daddy's presence became contagious not only for my sons, but it made me excited to come home and get in their presence. I left my frustration and exhaustion at work because I knew someone was eager to get into Daddy's presence. The excitement was so contagious that I fully expected my wife to come sliding across the floor next... that did not happen.

What if we were as excited to get into the presence of our Heavenly Father? Theologically I understand God is always present, but there is a difference when we intentionally run to the door and fall on our knees at his feet. I believe God gets excited when there is this joyous, urgent, sincere plea from us for his presence. If you need his presence in your life, I suggest you make it a priority, but you might have to beat me to the door because I got the boot!

You're Not College Material

*"Not one word of all the good promises that
the Lord had made to the house of Israel had
failed; all came to pass."*

Joshua 21:45

"You are not college material." Those are the very words a "Guidance Counselor" said to me many years ago at Wilson Middle School in Erie, Pennsylvania. As I write these words today, I can testify regardless of the counselor's assessment; God had other plans for me.

I can't lie. The counselor's words had stung me and made me question my abilities for years, and maybe it's why I took the long road to arrive at this point in my life. But, as the old saints would say, "I wouldn't take nothing for my journey now." I've seen God's grace, authority, and power become active in my life. I've seen His Word supersede that of man. You can't tell me what my God won't do! I know for myself how He can transform your life and destiny. I know for myself when God says you can, it really doesn't matter what anyone else has to say. I chose to embrace God's plan and purpose for my life rather than a man's opinion and limitations.

I wish I could run into that counselor today. I don't want to brag or boast, but I want to testify that my God is able! He is able to do exceedingly and abundantly above all you can ask or think. I don't know what God has promised in your life, but all I know is when man says no, God can still say yes.

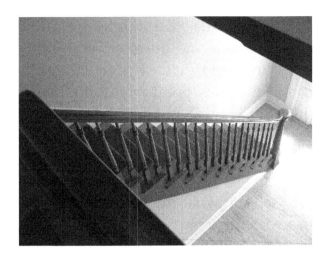

CALL ME

*"Call to Me, and I will answer you, and show
you great and mighty things, which you
do not know."*

Jeremiah 33:3

When we first moved into this house, we were relatively new parents. Our oldest was six years old, and our youngest, not yet born, would join us in two months. It was a two-story home with the master bedroom downstairs. My son was a little apprehensive about sleeping upstairs all alone, and to be truthful, I was a little nervous about leaving him up there. So, I placed a one-way monitor in his room, and I told him if he ever needed me, he could call me, and I would be right there (new parent). This was probably one of the biggest mistakes I ever made as a parent.

In the first two weeks, he'd put my words to the test. He'd call me, and I would dash upstairs to let him know I'd heard him. I would reassure him that I was always listening. He tested me. He'd call me in a loud voice, and other times he'd whisper. Regardless of how he called me, I had given my word that I would be right there if called. Sometimes my wife would have to wake me out of a sound sleep to let me know, "He's calling you again." I struggled to keep my word, but every time he called, I climbed those stairs because my word needed to count for something.

How much more will God keep his word to you? His word says, "I will answer them before they even call to me. While they are still talking about their needs, I will go ahead and answer their prayers!" (Is 65:24) I also hear the Lord saying, "Call to Me, and I will answer you, and I will tell you great and mighty things, which you do not know."

Well, as my son tested me, the only thing I can tell you today is to put God to the test. Call on Him. You might even whisper His name, and he declares he'll answer your call. I hear my mother singing, "Call him up and tell'em what you want."

STOP PRETENDING

"The Lord is close to all who call on Him, yes, to all who call on Him in truth."

Psalm 145:18

I hate getting sick. I rarely acknowledge the clearly visible signs that I am not at my best. I try to push through it. I hate to cancel a commitment I've made because I have a little sniffle, so I will ignore it and pretend nothing is wrong. I am reminded on the job that I have sick days and should use them, but that would mean I'd have to acknowledge that I'm sick.

My wife watches me go through this tortured ritual until she finally says, "I made an appointment for you; it's in the morning." I usually reply, "But I'm good!" To make her happy, I'll show up at the appointment to prove there's nothing wrong with me.

The next morning the doctor asks, "What's going on with you today?" To which I reply, "My wife thinks I'm sick. I've been sneezing, coughing, and I have a little fever, but I'm good." The doctor says, "So, you've been sneezing, coughing, with a fever; I can see you're congested, and your throat is pretty red. Let's stop pretending; your symptoms normally mean you're sick, so let me prescribe you something to help you get better."

I heard someone say, "God can't heal who we pretend to be." We can pretend like everything is well and "we're good," but the truth is we're hurting inside. If we are to receive our healing, we must stop pretending and get before the Great Physician and tell him our real condition, so he can prescribe just what we need to help us get better.

How Long Will You Stay There?

*"Moses My servant is dead. Now therefore,
arise, go over this Jordan, you and all this
people, to the land which I am giving to them—
the children of Israel. Every place that the sole
of your foot will tread upon I have given you, as
I said to Moses."*

Joshua 1:2-3

Have you ever been paralyzed by inde-
cision and watched precious time
slip away because you failed to take
a step? I mean, you could see the path and

direction you should go, but uncertainty and fear prevented you from moving forward. When we fail to take that step forward, we find ourselves in the same place, in the same position, complaining about the same thing to the same people in a different year.

I was talking with a friend the other day, and I could see so many great things God had in store for him. He spoke about his goals and aspirations, so I finally asked, "How long will you stay on this side of the river?" Much like in the story of Joshua, the promises God has for us is on the other side of the river. What God has for you is on the other side of the river of uncertainty, self-doubt, fear, criticism, and the anxieties over what others will think. Will you let those things thwart what God wants to do in your life?

The question becomes: Can you trust God enough to accept what he has for you? You have to get to the other side. God promised Joshua every place he stepped belonged to him, and he would prosper. The promise was beyond his comprehension, and it extended way beyond what he could physically see; it was beyond the river. I know you can't see it right now, and it seems a little scary, but move forward. Joshua had to do a few things: recognize God was with him, be strong and courageous, and TAKE ANOTHER STEP. It's time to move. Don't be afraid or dismayed for the Lord Your God is with You. So, in the words of the main character from the 1990s sitcom *Martin*, "Get to steppin!"

THE STRUGGLE IS WORKING FOR YOUR GOOD

Co-author Carla Barnett

*"We also rejoice in our suffering because we
know that suffering produces perseverance;
perseverance, character; and character, hope."*

Romans 5:3-4

It is evident by scrolling through social media that various celebrations are happening on any given day. There are birthdays, anniversaries, arrivals of babies, graduations, promotions, weight loss, holidays, and the list goes on. With all these celebrations, it can be easy to overlook the struggle that happened before the celebration. Sometimes we can feel like something is wrong with us because our social media seems absent from all the celebrations and dinner parties like everyone else. The truth of the matter is everyone struggles.

What we don't see on social media is the sleepless nights and nausea the comes with the pregnancy. We know the cap and gown ceremony, but not the failed assignments or the late nights to finish the makeup work. We can see the gym body, but often it came with a demanding diet and strenuous exercise routine. The promotion celebration came with tears after being passed over the year before. What we often see on Facebook is the result of a struggle, and social media highlights the celebration after a difficult struggle. There is nothing wrong with you with your life; you're just in the middle of the process.

Today may not be your day of celebration, but a day full of struggle. I want to encourage you to hang in there because your time of celebration is on the way. Don't quit; instead, work through the frustration and disappointment. Persevere with purpose, knowing that the struggle is working for your good. Somewhere

I read, "We also rejoice in our suffering because we know that suffering produces perseverance; perseverance, character; and character, hope." Don't let struggle stop you from your Divine Purpose. The greater the struggle, the greater the celebration. Your day of Celebration is on the way.

REFLECTIONS

CHAPTER 2

ECHOES OF RESILIENCY

*"For though the righteous
fall seven times, they
rise again…"*

Proverbs 24:16 NIV

THE FERN

"I will make them and the places all around My hill a blessing; and I will cause showers to come down in their season; there shall be showers of blessing."

Ezekiel 34:26

"Hey, Chaplain, let me show you something; you'd like this," she said as she reached for her iPad. A young lady I had met several times in the Cancer Center was here again for another round of chemo. Over the months, we've talked about faith and where she gains strength to help her during these times. She told me she gains most of her strength from encountering God through nature and taking walks to enjoy flowers and wildlife. So, I was not surprised when she opened her iPad to show me some of the most beautiful plants and flowers in her backyard.

However, I was a little surprised when she stopped on the picture she wanted me to see. I saw a tree, and it seemed to be dry and dying. I said, "That's interesting; what am I looking at exactly?" I asked this in the hopes she could help me understand the significance of the picture she was showing me. She pointed to the plant around the tree, which again appeared dry, brittle, and dying. She told me to wait, and then she swiped the photo to the left, and the same plant was pictured, though now a beautiful vibrant green.

She said, "It's called a Resurrection Fern. It just needs rain, and it comes back to life." Now, I had all kinds of preaching points swirling in my head, but I asked, "How does that speak to you?" What she said next blessed me in a great way. She said, "It says to me it's not over. It may look like it's hopeless, and it may look dead, but it just needs a little rain." Her eyes welled with tears, as she was speaking to her condition. I looked at her and just affirmed her confession, and said, "You're right it's not over. Let's trust God through the rain because I believe there is a resurrection coming soon."

Have you ever noticed children love to run through the rain, but as adults, we do our best to avoid it? Perhaps a little rain could bring life back to that dry and desperate situation in your life.

HAVE YOUR WAY, LORD. REALLY?

*"Not that we are sufficiently qualified in our-
selves to claim anything as coming from us, but
our sufficiency and qualifications come from
God. He has qualified us [making us sufficient]
as ministers of a new covenant [of salvation
through Christ], not of the letter [of a written code] but of the Spirit; for the letter [of the
Law] kills [by revealing sin and demanding
obedience], but the Spirit gives life."*

2 Corinthians. 3:5-6

Gospel singer Anita Wilson has a song
where she sings, "Lord, I don't mind.
I would like for you to just have your

way. It's alright. I would like for you to just have your way." It is a beautiful song, and tears rush to my eyes almost every time I hear it. The lyrics are simple, but its virtue is challenging to live out. If I can be transparent for a moment, I've found in my life that my desire and His way are often in conflict. Sometimes, I want my way.

My desire and His way are often in conflict because God is trying to grow me up, but I'm comfortable in my current position. I'm comfortable because growing up can be a painful process. Maturing means you may have to go through some hardship or pain, but through these trials, we discover the Lord's ultimate purpose is to bring us joy and hope, and conform us to be like Jesus (2 Cor. 3:18).

It is just unfortunate that we rarely mature when things are easy. We seem to learn our best lessons through struggle. We learn to be cautious of the hot stove only after suffering the injury of a burn. Someone may ask: Why does God allow us to experience so much hardship or pain?

Charles Stanley writes, "God allows hardship in order to reveal His character, love, and power. During life's storms, people who cling to their heavenly Father will find Him trustworthy and real."

No one wants to suffer, experience pain or sorrow, but it helps us to grow up. Hardship, though we dislike it, causes us to become mature believers who are more like Christ. Since we are qualified by God and not ourselves, in the middle of it all, as mature believers we declare, "Sovereign God, you're in control, and Lord, I don't mind if you will just have your way."

I HAVE ONE MORE SHOUT!

"Then Jesus shouted, 'Father, I commit my spirit to you,' and with those words he died."

Luke 23:46

Imagine Jesus on the cross in pain and agony as his lungs are collapsing, struggling to breathe. Amid his pain, he manages to give one last shout. He struggles, but he shouts, "Father into thy hands, I commend my spirit!"

Even while dying, Jesus gives an illustrative lesson that even in our struggles, we ought to have a shout in us. A shout of joy. A shout of confidence. A shout of divine expectation. A shout that declares, Lord, whatever comes I'm putting it in your hands.

As I look at my life, many times, I've witnessed that my struggle gave birth to my shout. Maybe, you can look back over your life and testify to the same experience. As you look back now, you can observe, if you hadn't gone through certain experiences, you wouldn't be where you are today. If you hadn't gone through the struggle, you couldn't lift your voice right now and shout thank you to the Lord!

As I look over my life, I confess the Lord has been good to me; I wouldn't change anything, but it hasn't always been easy. In the toughest of times, like when we lost a child, we held on to God's hand, and eventually, the pain gave birth to praise. Maybe you can testify, like me, wounds ultimately gave birth to your worship, bruises gave birth to blessing, and yes, struggles gave birth to my shout! So, excuse me if it seems strange to you, but I understand maybe you don't know our story. If we are followers of Christ, we strive to learn from him in every situation, and Jesus teaches us with his last earthly utterance to shout to the Lord, regardless of the struggle. I don't know about you, but I still have one more shout!

GET UP AND GO LIGHT IT!

"Jesus said to him, 'Rise, take up your bed and walk.' And immediately the man was made well, took up his bed, and walked. And that day was the Sabbath."

John 5: 8-9

Author Sara Henderson penned the following sentiment concerning the strength a person possesses. She said, "Don't wait for a light at the end of a tunnel, stride down there and light the bloody thing yourself."

Henderson's call to action provokes us to move from a state of paralysis and trust the strength we possess and move forward. I've discovered that sometimes it just takes a word to help us move forward. Jesus challenged a man who had been lying on a mat for 38 years with these words: "Would you like to get well?" (John 5:6 NLT) Really? Why ask this question? I think Jesus asked the question because, like this man, we can sometimes become comfortable living with and being defined by the issues in our lives.

The Amplified Bible says the man had a "deep-seated and lingering disorder" for 38 years. We don't know precisely the issue, but we know he was sick or incapacitated. His illness robbed him of his strength and ability. Whatever it was, it was deep-seated and lingering, a deadly combination. I wonder about all of the things he'd missed over those 38 years. Did he miss the joy of his family? Did he miss the laughter and smiles of his children? Did he miss establishing real friendships because he let his issues linger? What a sad condition to find yourself when we allow problems linger. What are you missing because you allow things to linger?

I'm so glad that no matter how long we've been in our condition, the right word from the right source can change everything. Lying on a comfortable mat, satisfied with life frozen in time, Jesus speaks, "Rise, pick up your mat and walk." Perhaps these words are the right words for you today; get up and go light the bloody thing!

BOUNCE BACK

"Now the Lord said to Samuel, "How long will you grieve over Saul, since I have rejected him from being king over Israel? Fill your horn with oil and go; I will send you to Jesse the Bethlehemite, for I have selected a king for Myself among his sons."

1 Samuel 16:1

I saw a billboard today that read, "Life begins when you get back up." If you've ever made a mistake, welcome to the club. Here's a quick news flash: We're all part of the same, flawed human race, and we make mistakes. Lord knows I've had my share of mistakes, but our flaws or mistakes should never get the last word about who we are as individuals.

Our mistakes, flaws, or the losses we suffer do not define the totality of our character. What defines our character is the way we bounce back from those mistakes. The Lord asked Samuel, "How long will you grieve, Saul?" He goes on to say, "Fill your horn with oil and go." In other words, the Lord said, it's time to bounce back.

Maybe yesterday did not turn out as expected, but today you get a chance to bounce back. Fill your horn with oil and move forward. The horn represents authority and power, and the oil represents healing. God supplies the authority, power, and the healing you need to get up from your past, acknowledge the flaws, and begin life again. I believe there is a bounce back in your story.

MORE THAN ENOUGH

*"Therefore, humble yourselves under the mighty
hand of God, that He may exalt you at the
proper time, casting all your anxiety on Him,
because He cares for you."*

1 Peter 5:6-7

Have you ever felt the task was too big for you? Have you ever wrestled with uncertainty and self-doubt? Well, you're not alone; I've been there myself. All of us have those moments because we are human. When you consider it, there is not a whole lot to us, and as human beings, we're pretty fragile. But God can take something fragile and seemingly insignificant and do something great with it. In the right hand, small, fragile things can do great work.

You might recall God took a small boy and a fragile insignificant little sling and slew a fierce giant. In the right hands, a boy's seemingly insignificant snack lunch can feed thousands. In the right hands, Jesus took twelve weak and seemingly insignificant men and changed the world forever. If God can use a child's toy sling, a boy's lunch, and twelve strong-headed men, think what great things he can do with you. If we dare place our fragile lives in the hand of this great God, we will discover we are more than enough for him to do great things.

Hey, just in case you did not know, or perhaps you needed to be reminded, you're more than enough in the hands of the Lord. So, go out and conquer the day.

REFLECTIONS

CHAPTER 3

ECHOES OF SECURITY

"Safety does not depend on our conception of the absence of danger. Safety is found God's presence, in the center of His perfect will."

T.J. Bach

WHEN THE WOLFHOUNDS ARE AFTER YOU

"But let all those rejoice for joy because You defend them; Let those also who love Your name be joyful in you. For You, O Lord, will bless the righteous; with favor you will surround him as with a shield."

Psalm 5:11-12

One day, my youngest son asked if he could go to our neighbor's house to see a friend. I gave him my permission and watched as he walked down the street to knock on the door. Everything seemed good as he walked the few paces to talk to his friend, but I did not know our neighbor had a couple of massive dogs.

As the neighbor's child opened the door, two huge animals, the size of miniature horses, came bursting through the door and gave chase to my son. I've never seen my son move with such speed. He came barreling toward me with two Great Danes mixed with Wolfhound in hot pursuit. As he raced toward me, the only thing he managed to get out of his mouth was, "DAADDDYYY!"

My first thought was that they were going to eat him up (don't judge me). Somehow, he managed to outrun these two massive dogs, and he jumped into my chest and spun onto my back all in one motion.

Now, all I saw were these two miniature horses galloping toward me. My very next thought was that, now, they were going to eat me up. I was okay with the prospect of being eaten because I knew I could handle the pain better than my son. Fortunately, neither of us had to endure pain because as soon as my son jumped into my arms, the dogs turned and went the other way.

Well, such is our lives. Wolfhounds seem to burst into our lives out of nowhere, but the good thing is Daddy is still watching. Like my son, you may not be able to pray a long prayer, but if you can manage to yell "DADDY!" and run towards him, I guarantee there is safety in his arms. The things that chase you can seem intimidating, vicious, and overwhelming, but when they come face to face with your Heavenly Father, they instantly become small, insignificant, and have to turn and run in the opposite direction.

GOD BLOCKED IT.

"But now thus says the Lord, he who created you, through the rivers, O Jacob, he who formed you, O Israel, "Fear not, for I have redeemed you; I have called you by name, you are mine. 2 When you pass through the waters, I will be with you; and through the rivers, they shall not overwhelm you; when you walk through the fire you shall not be burned, and the flames shall not consume you. For I am the Lord your God, the Holy One of Israel, your Savior."

Isaiah 43:1-3a

D id you have a chance to watch a couple of football games this past weekend? Did you see that play? No, not the great catch or the long run, I'm talking about that block! Sometimes we get so excited by the endzone dance that we forget it all started with a block.

Well, in a way, our lives can resemble a football game. We can get so excited and focused on running toward the goal line that we can forget to thank God for blocking for us and preventing unforeseen trouble from coming into our lives.

If you took an inventory of your life, you know you haven't been that good, but thank God for his favor. A songwriter said it best: "Haven't lived a perfect life, seems I've done wrong more than I've done right. But thank God for compassion and forgiveness that kept me from a terrible plight. God blocked it; He wouldn't let it be so." Is that your testimony? It certainly is mine.

The enemy has a desire and a plan to kill you, but God keeps blocking for us. Our opponent tried to blindside and steal our joy, but

God blocked it. If the enemy could, he would destroy you, oh, but God is our weak side and strong side blocker! Often, we get a chance to celebrate some of the successes in our lives and maybe dance in the endzone a little bit, but we ought to take a few moments and thank God because he keeps blocking for us.

Peace in the Storm

"My help comes from the Lord, who made heaven and earth. He will not let your foot be moved; he who keeps you will not slumber. Behold, he who keeps Israel will neither slumber nor sleep."

Psalm 121: 2-4

The other night I slept well. I didn't hear a thing. I woke up the next morning, and to surprise, my smartphone is full of warnings about the danger of tornadoes, thunderstorms, and flash flooding. I had no idea of all these things happening outside my window. While the storm was raging, I slept in perfect peace.

I don't know what storm you're going through right now, but I do know the one who can keep you in the middle of your storm. The Bible declares, "The Lord is your keeper; the shade at your right hand." In other words, He knows how to protect you and keep you cool when the world tries to turn the heat up in your life. When storms rage all around us, I am so glad we have a God who knows how to speak to each one.

The beautiful thing about our God is that He'll watch over us when we can't watch over ourselves. The Bible declares, "He'll never slumber, nor will He sleep." God always has his eye on you, so let the storm rage, and rest in the comfort that God knows how to keep you and give you peace right in the middle of the storm.

REDEEMED

"O give thanks to the LORD, *for He is good;*
For His compassion and loving kindness
endure forever! Let the redeemed of the LORD
say so, Whom He has redeemed from the hand
of the adversary."

Psalm 107: 1-2

W hen I was a child, I can recall my friends and I walking down the street collecting old soda bottles, or as we call it in Pennsylvania, old pop bottles. We would collect these bottles because someone had tossed them aside and considered them trash. The bottles would be drained of their contents, left on the side of the road, and covered with dirt. Regardless of their condition, we would still pick them up because we knew they still had value.

We were smart enough to read the tiny print at the bottom of the bottle that said, "redeemable." The maker of the bottle wrote on the bottle that the bottle was worth five cents. Oh, yeah. If we were willing to reach down in the dirt and pick it up, we could exchange the bottle because it was still worth something. I knew if I could find two bottles, I could swap the bottle at the corner store for a 10-cent pack of Lemon Heads, or Boston Baked Beans, all because the bottle still had value.

Listen, I don't know if you've ever felt tossed aside, drained of everything in you, and left like no one cared, but I keep reading in God's word that he is a Redeemer. He's written in large print that you have value because he made you in his very image. He is willing to wade through all kinds of dirt and pick you up, clean you off, and refill you until you overflow with his love and purpose. Why? Because you're still worth it.

You are not alone. We all need redemption. We're all dirty, but I'm so glad God loves us so much that he is still willing to pick us up no matter what pile of dirt we find ourselves stuck in. For the Bible says, "Let the redeemed of the LORD say so, Whom He has redeemed from the hand of the adversary." I'm glad He redeemed me, and he'll do the same for you.

HEART CATHETERIZATION

"I the LORD *search the heart and examine the*
mind, to reward each person according to their
conduct, according to what their deeds deserve."

Jeremiah 17:10

I had a small heart procedure the other day, and I am pleased to report all is well. The doctor wanted to do this particular procedure because the previous test had proven inconclusive. He could tell my heart wasn't functioning optimally but couldn't figure out why.

I protested a little. I said, "I feel great; I'm exercising. I don't think there is anything wrong." However, the doctor replied, "Well, we can sometimes fool ourselves when it comes to the heart." He continued, "The only real way to tell what's going on with the heart is to go inside of it and take a look at it." He said, "It can be something really good or really bad, but we won't know until we get in there."

How often do we fool ourselves into thinking that we can examine our own heart? Sometimes, we measure our spiritual heart by the things we do or restrain ourselves from doing. We measure our hearts by what we say or refrain from saying. Well, just like our physical heart, our spiritual heart cannot be measured from the outside, nor by the things we're doing or not doing. The heart must be examined from the inside.

The good news is we have a doctor who specializes in performing Spiritual Heart Catheterizations. For the Bible declares, even though the heart is deceitful and wicked, "I, the Lord, search the heart, I test the mind, to give every man according to his ways, According-ing to the fruit of his doings." Well, today, let me encourage you, let the Lord examine your heart.

SILENT SATURDAY

"Therefore order the tomb to be made secure until the third day, lest his disciples go and steal him away and tell the people, 'He has risen from the dead,' and the last fraud will be worse than the first." Pilate said to them, "You have a guard of soldiers. Go, make it as secure as you can."

Matthew 27: 64-65

We know about Good Friday, and we rejoice on Resurrection Sunday, but the day in the middle is often forgotten. It is called Holy Saturday by some, but today I want to trademark it as Silent Saturday. We often overlook this day, possibly because we are uncomfortable with silence. Sometimes in the silence, we start to see all of the obstacles in front of us, and if we are not careful, fear can overtake our faith.

Under the silence of the night, the disciples saw Jesus arrested in a garden, and they fled for their lives (Matt26:56). From a distance, the disciples, except for John, watched in silence as they crucified my Savior (Lk 23:49). I can imagine they saw Jesus' lifeless body, as they took him off that tree and laid his body in another man's tomb. The thunderous sound of silence must have overwhelmed the disciples as they wiped away the tears when they saw the stone rolled in front of the tomb.

Yes, silence can be uncomfortable, but I am writing to you today to tell you that even in a quiet place, God is still at work. Jesus reminds us, "My father is still working, and I am working too" (John 5:17 CEB). In the stunned silence of the room, as Jesus washed the disciples' feet, He said, "You don't understand what I'm doing now, but you will understand later" (John 13:7).

Listen, maybe you're experiencing a silent Saturday in your life right now, and perhaps you've been here a while. People may have left you high and dry, and maybe there are significant obstacles in your path, and perhaps it looks like there is no way you can come back from this one, but you're still here. They may have thrown dirt on you and declared it was over. Well, I have news to tell you. God is always at work, and before a rose can bloom, it has to take root in some dirt, so hold on – Sunday is on the way.

"ACTIVELY DYING"

" Yet you do not know [the least thing] about what may happen in your life tomorrow. [What is secure in your life?] You are merely a vapor [like a puff of smoke or a wisp of steam from a cooking pot] that is visible for a little while and then vanishes [into thin air]."

James 4:14 (AMP)

Recently, I've had the privilege of working as a Chaplain in a hospital here in San Antonio. In the hospital environment, you become familiar with specific terms and phrases. One phrase that I've become familiar with: "actively dying." The hospital uses this phrase when a person is in the last moments of their life. In these moments, the hospital calls for a Chaplain to come share words of encouragement, pray for and with the individual, comfort the family, extend faith, and represent the presence of God in the room.

"Actively dying" is a pretty strange phrase when you consider it because we're all actively dying. Scripture reminds us that this life is but a vapor. We are here just for a moment like a mist from a water bottle that cools us on a hot summer day.

We are actively dying. Since this is the case, we should call on one another, sharing words of encouragement, praying and comforting each other, extending our faith, and representing our Father wherever we find ourselves because we're in a crisis; we are actively dying. It is a strange phrase, but one I've become pretty acquainted with over the last few years, as loved ones have passed away. I didn't always make it to the hospital room to have a final conversation because I didn't want to acknowledge that we are all "actively dying," but we are. So, since we are actively dying, the question becomes: "What will you do with today?" Who will you call on, and who will you trust in this crisis moment? I suggest you call on the one who has a home for you beyond this place. I suggest you call on the Lord.

REFLECTIONS

CHAPTER 4

ECHOES OF GRACE

"Your worst days are never so bad that you are beyond the reach of God's grace. And your best days are never so good that you are beyond the need of God's grace."

Jerry Bridges

Background Noise

"I wait quietly before God, for my victory comes from him. Let all that I am wait quietly before God, for my hope is in him. 6 He alone is my rock and my salvation, my fortress where I will not be shaken."

Psalm 62:1, 5-6

My wife and I were looking for a home to purchase. As we were looking at this particular house, we noticed a problem. A train, with several cars, came roaring through the back yard with all of the noise of clanging tracks, bells, and horns. The train ran right behind the house we came to view. The seller noticed us standing in the front yard and came running over and said, "Don't worry about that train, you'll get used to it; after a while, it just becomes background noise."

We laughed a little and got back in the car. We had seen enough. Who wants to live with background noise? Sadly, we live in a world with a lot of background noise, and like the seller of this home, we adapt to the noise, and it doesn't bother us anymore. We are so accustomed to the noise in our lives that sometimes it becomes difficult for us to function without it. We become uncomfortable with silence. We need the television on, even if we're not watching it. We need the music playing even if we're not listening to it. All of this noise makes it difficult for us to hear anything. When we become comfortable with tuning out the background noise, like the seller of this house, it becomes difficult for us to hear the important things because we've taught ourselves to stop listening.

Have you ever really considered how noisy your life is? Perhaps God is trying to get your attention, but the noise in your life is so loud you can't hear Him. Whenever Jesus had an important decision to make, he left the crowd, got away from the noise, found a place to himself, and prayed. In a quiet place, Jesus connected with the Father and found assurance, peace, and direction. Today I encourage you not to allow all the noise of life to drown out God's voice. It's time to turn down the noise, so you can hear what Daddy is saying.

I'D RATHER HAVE JESUS

"And if it be evil in your eyes to serve the Lord, choose this day whom you will serve… But as for me and my house, we will serve the Lord."

Joshua 24:15

Years ago, Kirk Franklin sang in a song, "I'd rather have Jesus than silver or gold." In the abstract, I think most believers would agree with the sentiments of those lyrics, but most of us don't have to make that choice every day. We don't choose between a pot of gold and the Prince of Peace in the literal sense, but every day we must choose to either follow Christ or our selfish desires.

It is so much easier to go off and give someone a piece of your mind, rather than to seek compromise and understanding. Every day, we make choices that reflect who we are as believers in Christ. Life is so much tougher than these song lyrics because every day, we must consciously choose to follow His ways and not our own. Choosing his way is not always easy, but I can promise it is worth it.

So today, God gives another day of grace, and we receive another conscious opportunity to choose whom we will serve. Self or Savior? We can choose to forgive someone or hold on to bitterness. We get to choose to be generous to someone, or selfish. We get a choice to show the love of Christ or the cold indifference that breaks faith with our fellow human beings. Today, I pray you'll choose to declare, "As for me, I will serve the Lord!" Our faith is more than the lyrics of a song. The choice we make in this life is a declaration: "I'd rather have Jesus more than anything."

Senior Moments

"For you died [to this world], and your [new, real] life is hidden with Christ in God."

Colossians 3:3 (AMP)

Have you ever hidden something so well that you couldn't find it yourself? I am finding as I get older, I have these moments more and more often. Funny, lately, I can't seem to locate stuff even when I'm not trying to hide it. Some have called this, "having a senior moment."

Well, in a similar way, as we mature in Christ, we ought to have some senior moments. We should hide some things so well in Christ that we forget where we placed it. The Bible suggests we hide our very lives in Christ. We should hide our lives so well in Christ that it is difficult to find our old selves.

Have you ever had a senior moment that surprised you? You had an incident at work that would usually cause you to react with anger, but this time you responded with grace – a senior (mature) moment. As we mature in Christ, senior moments should occur more and more often. We should be so well hidden in Christ that we can't find that old corrosive attitude. We can't find that destructive anger. We've had a senior moment, and we are no longer able to find the deceitful person we used to be. We are made new in Christ. We are in him, and we are no longer the same. In Christ, we are a new creation. So, let me encourage you today to have a senior moment.

THE NAIL
Co-author Carla Barnett

"You were dead in sins, and your sinful desires were not yet cut away. Then he gave you a share in the very life of Christ, for he forgave all your sins, and blotted out the charges proved against you, the list of his commandments which you had not obeyed. He took this list of sins and destroyed it by nailing it to Christ's cross."

Colossians 2:13-14

A s we were preparing to take a trip out of town, my son notices a nail sticking out of one of the tires. I was a little frustrated and angry because a 25-cent nail had the potential to delay or cancel our plans. We quickly drove to a tire shop around the corner from our house. The store was closed, but the door was still open. Side note: Have you ever just thanked God for the open doors in your life? I told the gentleman about my problem, and he told me that although they were closed, he would take a look at the tire.

As he examined the tire, he said, "not good." The nail damaged the tire in such a way that it was not repairable. We needed a new tire. I told him of our plans to drive out of town, so he examined all of the tires. The gentleman suggested we replace every single one. Then he said something that stuck with me. He said, "Thank God for the nail because it brought you in. You wouldn't want to drive out of town with those tires. It would be too dangerous." A 25-cent nail delayed our plans but possibly saved us from unseen danger. So, as I thought about that cheap nail lodged my tire, I reflected on how thankful I felt for some other inexpensive nails.

The three nails that were lodged in my Savior's body as he hung on the cross to save humanity for eternity. Lord, I'm thankful!

His sacrifice replaced my frustration and anger with joy, peace, unconditional love, and gratitude.

One little rusty, 25-cent nail had the power to cause destruction or even death, but three nails had the power to bring us life more abundantly. Don't allow a nail situation to deflate the plans God has for your life. Don't count your delay as denial; it just might be that the nail is working for your good, so that you can move into your ordained destiny.

The nails are no longer holding our Savior on the cross. He has risen and reigns forever, and he'll reign in your life if you let him. Rom 8:28

END PIECES

*"For everything, there is a season and a time
for every matter under heaven:"*

Ecclesiastes 3:1

My mother never let anything go to waste. As children, junk my siblings and I found no use for she'd find a way to re-purpose. I can hear her now saying, "Don't throw that away; somebody might need that." In our minds, we thought: *Who in the world would want something like that?* As children, maybe you were like my siblings and me; we could not figure out the purpose for the end pieces to a loaf of bread. I still need someone to tell me the purpose of the end piece.

We would always reach past the end piece to get to the real bread. In our minds, there was absolutely no reason to include these undesirable, unusable, and unwanted slices of bread. We would call the loaf complete when the end pieces met together at the bottom of the bag. However, Mom would say, "Don't throw those pieces away." She had a plan for even those pieces.

She would take the end pieces and freeze them, and when she had enough of them, she'd make something new out of them. She'd take those end pieces and mix them with some eggs, milk, butter, cinnamon, sugar, a little vanilla (never raisins), and throw it in the oven to make the best bread pudding you'd ever wanted to taste. We thought those end pieces were unusable, unwanted, and undesirable, but once them had gone through the heat, everyone wanted them.

Listen, life can sometimes make you feel like the end piece of a loaf of bread. You may feel undesirable, unwanted, misused, and picked over, but God has great plans for you. God, just like my mother, doesn't waste anything. The

Bible declares he even bottles your tears. The heartbreak we have experienced feels like an end piece. The job lost feels like an end piece but hold on and watch what God can make out of the end pieces. God is not a wasteful God. The breath he gave you today is by design, so use it for his glory. I know you may not see it right now, but the heat you are going through is working for your good!

THERE'S SOMETHING IN YOU

"And I will pray the Father, and He will give
you another Helper, that He may abide with
you forever— ¹⁷ *the Spirit of truth, whom*
the world cannot receive, because it neither sees
Him nor knows Him; but you know Him, for
He dwells with you and will be in you."

John 14:16-17

Everything came to a standstill as a draw-bridge rose; I assumed a large ship or yacht was passing and had caused the traffic from both the east and west sides of the bridge to come to a halt. I jogged to the top of the bridge to look, and to my surprise, I found it wasn't a large ship at all, but a little boat.

I asked an older gentleman standing next to me why they lifted the bridge for such a small boat. It was apparent the man was not a sailor because he replied, "Because it's got that tall thang in it." Now I'm not a sailor, but even I knew the tall thing he was referring to was called a mast. However, I liked the man's point: The little boat had something unmistakable in it. What the boat had in it could be seen from a distance, it made people stop and take notice, and barriers were removed because of what the little boat had in it.

Jesus declares that we have a Helper who not only dwells with us but lives in us (John 14:16-17). People may not see much when they look at you, and you may not even think highly of yourself, but they'll have to take notice because of the one who lives within you. Listen, because of the one in you, drawbridges will open, and the enemy can only watch you walk by in victory. People will wonder how such a little boat commands such respect, and someone will have to explain to them it is because of the one who lives in them.

Evening *Echoes*

REFLECTIONS

Evening *Echoes*

REFLECTIONS

CHAPTER 5

ECHOES OF ASSURANCE

"Joy is the settled assurance that God is in control of all the details of my life, the quiet confidence that ultimately everything is going all right, and the determined choice to praise God in all things."

Kay Warren

LET THE SON SHINE IN.

"Rather, you must grow in the grace and knowledge of our Lord and Savior Jesus Christ. All glory to him, both now and forever! Amen."

2 Peter 3:18

A friend of mine let me borrow his bow saw to cut down some branches in my backyard. When I say branches, you should really picture huge trees in your mind. We'd allowed a couple of families to live in our home as the military took us around the country. Unfortunately, those families never trimmed the trees back. As a result, shade covered our entire yard, and the sun could not reach the ground. On the surface, this seems like an ideal situation for those hot days in Texas, until you looked at the ground.

Our backyard looked like a total wasteland, not a blade of grass in sight. As my wife would say, "The backyard is a hot mess." You see, we need some sun to shine on the ground for the grass to grow. So, with a little handheld bow saw, I went to work, cutting down what felt like half a forest. I cut enough back so the sun could shine on our ground. We needed the sun to give life back to our yard.

Similarly, we need to cut down those things that are blocking the SON from shining over the ground of our lives. Have you ever wondered why you're not growing in certain areas? Have you ever wondered why, even though every-thing is in place for growth, nothing seems to grow? Could it be we've blocked God out of that section of our life? Today, I challenge you to grab your bow saw and start cutting some things out of your life, and let the SON shine over your wasteland and grow in the grace and knowledge of Jesus Christ.

THE GREAT EXCHANGE

"To console those who mourn in Zion, To give them beauty for ashes,
The oil of joy for mourning, The garment of praise for the spirit of heaviness;
That they may be called trees of righteousness,
The planting of the Lord, that He may be glorified."

Isaiah 61:3

I spoke to a young mother who started giving her son a small allowance to teach him the value of money. The young man was excited to get an allowance, but he had yet to learn the value of each bill, so he was content to collect as many bills as possible, but he didn't pay much attention to the denomination on the bill. His older sister, on the other hand, understood the value and got the better of him by suggesting exchanges like two one-dollar bills for one five-dollar bill. He thought that was a pretty good exchange. He got two, and she got one. He wins! Since we understand the value and how it works, we know this was a pretty uneven exchange.

Similarly, we are the beneficiaries of the most uneven exchange ever recorded in history. God gave us His priceless Son in exchange for our worthless sin. The Prophet Isaiah, when announcing the Messiah's mission, describes this great exchange like this, "…beauty for ashes, the oil of joy for mourning, the garment of praise for the spirit of heaviness." We get His strength for our weakness and His salvation for our sin. What a great exchange!

All too often, like the young son trying to learn the difference between having much and having value, we tend to hang on to the things that are worthless in our lives when God has something of greater value for us. I challenge you to let go of those cheap things and grab hold of all that God has for you. Unlike the young man, when we enter into this exchange, we win.

HOLD ON TO YOUR CONFESSION

*"Yet in all these things we are more than
conquerors through Him who loved us. ³⁸ For
I am persuaded that neither death nor life, nor
angels nor principalities nor powers, nor things
present nor things to come, ³⁹ nor height nor
depth, nor any other created thing, shall be
able to separate us from the love of God which
is in Christ Jesus our Lord."*

Romans 8:37-39

What do you do when your confession and your condition collide, and your world seems to fall apart?

What do you do when your profession of faith runs into the enemies of hate? What do you do when your confession looks in doubt, and your haters ask, "Where is your God now?"

First, don't feel alone; know that our elder brother Jesus went through the same thing. The scoffers at the cross said, "He trusts in God; let God deliver him now if he desires him. For he said, 'I am the Son of God.'" The haters will ridicule and try to tear you down when life throws you some difficulties but know that God has a purpose beyond this present condition.

Secondly, know that the Father is on your side, and somehow this present suffering cannot be compared to the glory of God, which shall be revealed in us. I don't know how, but somehow, God is going to get glory out of this struggle! I believe the scripture is true when it says, "And we know, all things work together for good to them that love God, to them who are the called according to his purpose."

Finally, as difficult as it may be, hold on to your confession. We can celebrate the resurrection because Jesus did not allow his condition to confiscate his confession. I thank God, because Jesus held on to his confession, and now I have the right to come boldly to the Throne of Grace and find grace to help in the time of need. I encourage you today: Don't let your condition confiscate your confession because your confession is made unto salvation.

DESIGNATED DRIVER

"I will instruct you and teach you in the way
you should go; I will counsel you with
my eyes upon you."

Psalm 32:8

I am the designated driver for our family. If it's a trip across town or the country, I generally take responsibility for driving the family. However, on the occasions when my wife is driving, it's amazing how I see things along the way that I've never seen before. *How long has that been there?* I'd miss things that had always been there because I was so focused on the task of driving,

Well, our lives can be just like that trip across town or the country when we place ourselves in the driver seat. "We can be so focused on reaching our destination that we miss all of God's blessings along the way. I once heard Pastor Michael Steve Brown of San Antonio say, "We run the risk of becoming so accustomed to God's grace that we are no longer amazed by it." The statement rings true when we are solely focused on the task of the day and not on the one who made the day. Maybe, we've been in the driver's seat too long.

I never want to reach the point in my relationship with my Heavenly Father where I am no longer amazed. I want to be wonderstruck forever be his grace, mercy, and power. It might mean I have to relinquish the wheel of control in my life to Him, become the patient passenger and go wherever he leads me. Why don't you take a moment and get in the passenger seat, let God drive, and be amazed by His grace once again? It is grace that woke you up this morning, and it is amazing!

A Place Called Home
Co-author Carla Barnett

"In My Father's house are many mansions;
if it were not so, I would have told you. I go
to prepare a place for you. And if I go and
prepare a place for you, I will come again and
receive you to Myself; that where I am,
there you may be also."

John 14:2-3

I don't always like traveling because I have to take too much stuff with me. One winter, my family and I traveled from Texas to Erie, Pennsylvania. When we left Texas, the temperature was 65°, and when we landed, the temperature was 10°. Yes, it can be a shock to your system if you're not ready. The quick spiritual lesson learned from the trip was the further I got from home, the more things I had to wear and carry.

Before we left Texas, we were layered up, anticipating the cold. We carried winter coats, sweaters, and we wore our thermal underwear because we were flying home anticipating the weather. Wearing extra clothing and carrying baggage can be exhausting. Are you wearing and carrying excess weight because you're too far from home?

I discovered the closer I got to home, the more I took off. When we were leaving the East Coast, we were anticipating home, so we didn't wear the thermal clothing we'd brought with us. At the airport, we took off sweaters, winter caps, and gloves. The closer we got to a place called home, the more we pulled off.

Listen, the Lord has a place prepared for us, a place called home, and the closer we move towards home, the more we should pull off. You don't have to wear that shame anymore, so pull it off. You don't have to carry the anxieties, guilt, and disappointment of the past, so pull it off. Pull off that anger and bitterness; you don't need it because you're closer to a place called home. John 14: 1-6.

IN THE MEANTIME, KEEP LIVING.

"Build homes and plan to stay; plant vine-
yards, for you will be there many years. Marry
and have children, and then find mates for
them and have many grandchildren. Multiply!
Don't dwindle away!"

Jeremiah 29:1-12

What do you do when things don't turn out as you planned? What do you do when you have to stay in a place of disappointment longer than antici-pated? Have you ever been in that place where it goes from bad to worse? If not, my mother would say, "just keep living."

Every day, as a Hospital Chaplain, I work with patients whose lives have been transformed by some life-altering diagnosis or terminal disease. These living, breathing human documents teach me something new every day, lessons I could never learn from a textbook or seminary. One of the greatest lessons I've learned is that regardless of the doctor's diagnosis, just keep living.

I am privileged to hear about the gardens they're planting, the weddings they're planning, the grandchildren that bring them joy, the deep-sea fishing trips, their hopes and dreams, their faith, and the God they serve. In other words, despite the difficult diagnosis, they have decided to just keep living.

It reminds me of the time a prophet named Jeremiah told those captured by a king named Nebuchadnezzar that their captivity was going to last a minute (70 years to be exact) but to keep living.

The Lord says to them, amid their trouble, build houses, plant gardens, get married, have children, seek peace. In other words, keep living! How do we do keep living in the middle of great difficulty? We do it by knowing God has a plan for our life, and He will visit us and perform His good word. So, in the meantime, Keep Living.

REFLECTIONS

CHAPTER 6

ECHOES OF FAITH

"Faith is to believe in what you do not see; the reward of this faith is to see what you believe."

Saint Augustine

THE TROLLEY

"It was good for me to be afflicted, in order to learn your statutes."

Psalm 119:71

I spoke to an older gentleman who wanted to tell me how he started a Bible study. I am always interested in listening to people tell their stories and how they're exercising their faith, so immediately, I stopped to listen to him. If I can be honest, the way he started the story made me think he had forgotten the subject.

He talked about a classic car he'd loved and had for many years. He spoke about how the car made him feel when he sat behind the wheel. It was his pride and joy, and his primary means of getting back and forth to work. His car broke one day, and he had to use public transportation. He confessed he was not happy about having to use public transportation and a little disappointed with God. What was God doing? He went from owning a car to getting up early in the morning for a long bus ride, followed by another 30-minute trolley ride to get to work.

I listened patiently, but I didn't hear anything about a Bible study. I heard about the loss of a cherished car and a lament about public transportation, but nothing about a Bible study. However, my spiritual antennas went up when he said, "When I lost that car, it was a real blessing." He explained while he was disappointed, his 30-minute trolley ride gave him uninterrupted time to study his Sunday School lesson.

The passengers on the trolley were regulars, and they would see each other every day as they traveled to work. A woman noticed him studying and asked what he was reading every day. He explained that his 30-minute ride gave him time to review his Sunday School lesson.

She asked if she could study with him, so he agreed. The two of them started studying the Sunday School lesson together and talking about the word of God daily.

One day another passenger overheard part of their conversation and disagreed with some of their analysis of the text. The old man told him, "I don't mind you disagreeing, but if you're going to disagree, you have to bring your Bible because it's about the scripture and what it says, and not your opinion." Well, the man started bringing his Bible, and soon the old man found himself in front of the trolley leading the entire car in the study of God's word because his car had stopped working.

Eventually, the older man got another car and had to leave the Bible study he had initiated, but one day he ran into the woman who had asked him to share his lesson. He asked how things were going. She was excited to report that the study was still going on and had expanded to a second car. All of this happened because a man turned his disappointment and frustration into dedication and faith, and because of it, lives changed forever. What will you do with your disappointing and frustrating moments? I suggest the next time you feel disappointed or frustrated, look around to see what door God has opened for you and not focus so much on what you believe was taken away.

TURN IT INTO PRAISE

"This is the day the Lord has made. We will rejoice and be glad in it."

Psalm 118: 24

A story on the Today Show caught my attention. Carol and Willie Fowler had planned an elaborate, sophisticated wedding reception for their daughter, only to have it canceled six weeks before the ceremony. The invitations delivered, venues reserved, food purchased, but now only disappointment was left on the menu. What do you when bitter disappointment rocks your world?

The Fowlers decided to turn their problems into praise, and their disappointment into a display of God's grace. Instead of canceling the venue and losing the money they had already invested, they threw a party for more than 200 homeless people. The 200 guests found themselves sitting at an elegant reception with a four-course meal in front of them, and more importantly, they found someone to remind them they mattered, and someone cared about them.

The Fowlers looked past their problem and found a way to serve and bless others. Instead of concentrating on the hurt they felt, they decided to turn their stinging disappointment into an opportunity to serve others. We become a visual display of God's grace when we learn to honor him in the middle of our disappointment instead of throwing a pity party.

People ask, what is the purpose of pain? I don't have a satisfactory answer to this question just yet. However, I've discovered when problems arise, God does not want us to wallow in self-pity but instead find a way to turn those problems into praise. In every situation, there is a way to give God glory; we only need to look for it.

We all have problems, but can I ask you what kind of party will you throw today? I've made up in my mind; I'm going to throw a praise party because it's still the day the Lord has made, and I choose to rejoice and be glad in it! Ps 118:24

THANK YOU

*"I will give thanks to the Lord with all my heart; I will tell of all Your wonders.
I will be glad and exult in You; I will sing praise to Your name, O Most High."*

Psalm 9:1-2

Thank you, Lord, for one more day. When my eyes pop open in the morning, usually, the first words that come to mind are, 'Thank you for another day.' I'm wise enough to know every day is a gift from God, and if He gave me one more day, I understand he still has a purpose and plan for my life. Because I consider the day a gift from him, the very least I can do is say "thank you."

If someone gave me a gift, and I refused to acknowledge and appreciate them, that would be pretty disrespectful. Sometimes, in our hurried lives, we unintentionally treat God disrespectfully. We act as though we deserve His grace and mercy. The truth of the matter is we haven't been that good that we deserve or merit His grace. It is not your good looks, education, or your job that allowed you to see today, but it is only by the grace of God.

God kept us. God protected us. God provided for us and continues to gift us with His grace even when we forget to humble ourselves and say, "thank you." Over the years, I've learned to humble myself because I just believe it's far better for me to humble myself and acknowledge Him than to have the Lord humble me. Now, if you agree, say it with me: "Lord, I thank you for one more day."

FAITH IS A LANGUAGE.

*"Now faith is the substance of things hoped
for, the evidence of things not seen."*

Hebrews 11:1

Have you ever tried to learn a foreign language? It's one of the hardest things to do in life. Maybe you can recall the torture of trying to learn French, Spanish, or Italian as you were going through high school. I can't tell you how many brain cells I burned up learning Hebrew and Greek in seminary. I thought I would never understand either of the languages. I kept thinking I was too old to learn that stuff (I used another word, but that's another language).

Anyway, here's what I discovered about learning a new language. I had to stop comparing the new language to the one I already knew. I just had to immerse myself in the new experience. I had to think in Hebrew or Greek to understand the language better. I can also tell you how quickly your understanding leaves when you stop practicing what you have learned. Sometimes it's difficult to walk in faith when you haven't immersed yourself in the language. Faith is hard. It is especially hard when you have lived an evidence-based life. How's that working for you?

The question becomes, "How do I move from an evidence-based life to a life based on the evidence of things not seen?" Well, much like my Hebrew and Greek experience, you have to stop comparing what you think you know to the concepts you have yet to understand.

You have to dive in and immerse yourself in the power and authority of the one who loves you. You have to think faith, talk faith, and walk in faith. Faith must become your new language. Faith begins to say, "I don't know how, but I do know who!" Faith declares, "This too shall pass." Faith says, "No matter what, it looks like God still has me in the palm of His hand."

What's in You?

"You are of God, little children, and have overcome them, because He who is in you is greater than he who is in the world."

1 John 4:4

Someone said, "What lies behind us and what lies ahead of us are tiny matters compared to what lies within us."

I confess I can spend a lot of time thinking about how I could have done some things better in the past and can consume a lot of time thinking about my tomorrows. It's a strange place to be because if I'm not careful, I can allow my thoughts of yesterday and tomorrow to lead me into missing today.

I encourage you not to allow failures of the past to hinder where God is taking you. It's a tiny matter. Don't let the challenge of the future hinder you from what God wants to do through you because what he wants to do through you is a small matter to him. I know it looks big and intimidating, but compared to the God we serve it's tiny, and compared to the Holy Spirit that lives in us, it is a small thing.

He has given us another day. What will you do with it? I dare you to stand boldly, love fully, forgive yourself and others completely, trust God, and move forward.

You can move forward with confident assurance knowing if God called you to it, He has given you the power to endure and succeed because greater is He that is in you, than He that is in the world." I can't promise it will be easy, but I can guarantee He'll be with you, and remember, it is just a tiny matter compared to the power that is within us.

FAITH THAT SUBDUES

"Who by faith conquered kingdoms, performed acts of righteousness, obtained promises, shut the mouths of lions, [34] quenched the power of fire, escaped the edge of the sword, from weakness were made strong, became mighty in war, put foreign armies to flight."

Hebrews 11:33-34

Our faith should challenge us to take on efforts greater than ourselves. God does not give us faith to settle for those ventures that are comfortable. Our faith should stretch us to uncomfortable points. Jesus said, our faith should cause us to love our enemies and pray for those who persecute you. We need great faith to do that. Someone said, "Faith isn't faith until you have to hold on to it." Why do we need faith if we can handle every issue and answer every question on our own? Sometimes, we fool ourselves into believing we must have every answer before we can move forward. At times, we hesitate to move because we don't want to appear foolish if we make a mistake, but if we had every answer, why would we need faith?

I once told a friend when I was wrestling with a decision, "I don't know how, but I do know who." The mark of faith is to trust God amid uncertainty and accept the challenge to move forward toward a vision bigger than our ability to carry. A modern picture of a person of faith is one who is timid, mild, and soft-spoken, but this does not seem to fit the biblical image.

The scripture says, "Who through faith subdued kingdoms, worked righteousness, obtained promises, stopped the mouths of lions, quenched the violence of fire, escaped the edge of the sword, out of weakness were made strong, became valiant in battle, turned to flight the armies of the aliens." And all of this came by faith.

Faith calls on us to trust God in uncertainty, be courageous, and accept whatever challenge is set before us. Now, hold on to your faith and go take on the day.

REFLECTIONS

CHAPTER 7

ECHOES OF COMPASSION

"When you realize that you are deeply loved by God, it enables you to love deeply."

Marty Cauley

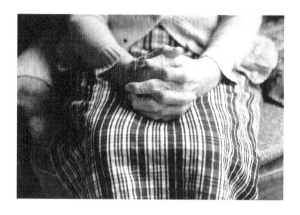

DIVINE APPOINTMENT

*"The Lord guides us in the way we should go
and protects those who please him."*

Psalm 37:23 (GNT)

I've had the pleasure of working as a hospital Chaplain and serving many of the veterans who have fought for the country. I've learned some incredible lessons from these veterans and expanded the scope of my ministry. I've had the extraordinary opportunity to minister to people who don't look like me or even think like me. One of the greatest lessons I learned came from a 92-year-old, female, World War II veteran.

As I walked into her room, I was a little apprehensive because I didn't know if we had anything in common. We came from different generations, different cultures, different ethnic backgrounds; what could we have in common? As I began to speak to her, she waved me closer because her hearing was not that good. I came close and knelt on the ground near her, and she asked for prayer.

As I concluded my prayer, she grabbed my hands and kissed them. At that moment, I knew I was in the right place. We often think about how different we are, but the truth of the matter is that we have more in common than we do differences. We are bound together by our common humanity, our need for someone to be with us when we're hurting, and we need someone to demonstrate the love of Christ. This veteran taught me a vital lesson: pain and suffering don't discriminate. We need each other, and we all need someone to pray for us. I came to see this encounter as a divine appointment meant to tear down some walls I didn't even know I had inside of me, and a chance to build new bridges. Every day, God gives us divine appointments. What will you do with yours?

LENDER OF HOPE

"Now may the God of hope fill you with all joy and peace as you believe so that you may overflow with hope by the power of the Holy Spirit."

Romans 15:13

Recently, I met a young man who reminded me why I do what I do. Hours removed from putting a semi-automatic rifle to his head and pulling the trigger, God gave me a divine appointment to cross his path and talk with him. This expert rifleman was at a loss to understand why the weapon he had operated for years did not go off and end his life. The very first words out of his mouth were, "Tell me about your God!"

What a great invitation, and one I don't often get so explicitly, but he could only attribute the recent events in his life to divine intervention and God Himself. Well, looking at the circumstances, I found quick agreement with him and asked him about the God he talked about and what he knew of Him. He said he had no relationship and knew nothing about God, but this incident led him to want to know more about Him. He asked me to explain the God I serve.

Once again, I marveled at the invitation. God had placed me in front of a person surrounded by a fog of hopelessness to share hope with him. At that moment, I became a lender of hope. As we spoke, I discovered this fog of hopelessness caused him to miss the brightness of his future: his wife, his children, his career, and everything he had going for him. His lack of hope had obscured everything in his life that was positive.

This young man needed hope desperately, and I had more than enough to share. I thought about my family, my faith, and everything that fills me with joy, and how quickly those things could change without hope. We talked for quite some time, and he asked me to share some scriptures with him, which I was happy to do. He wondered about how to receive the God we discussed. I walked him through some more scriptures, and I could see that it wasn't connecting. I asked him what he enjoyed, some of his interests, and I discovered he was in college studying theater. As he shared his interests, God gave me the following illustration to share with him.

I said, "Suppose we were going to the movies and you had no money, so I paid for your ticket. The only way you could get into the film is if you receive the ticket I purchased for you. You could say you don't deserve it, and your pride, guilt, and shame could compel you to refuse the ticket, but the only way to get in to see the movie is to receive the ticket I bought for you." I went on, speaking to this young man, "Christ has done the same thing for you. He has paid the price and purchased your ticket. All we have to do is just receive it." When I prayed and left him that day, I could hear him murmuring the phrase, "just receive the ticket." I had no idea at that moment if my time with him was fruitful, but at least I was able to lend him some hope.

By chance, I happened to run into the young man many months later. He was with his wife and baby daughter. He introduced me to his family and then told me, "I got the ticket. And man, I've been telling everybody about the ticket!" His hope had been restored.

I've discovered hope is transferable, and I want to be a lender of hope because I have plenty to spare. My hope is in the Eternal One. His name is Jesus. Today, I pray that you're able to be a Lender of Hope because someone needs it.

GONE FISHING

"Then He said to them, "Follow Me, and I will make you fishers of men."

Matthew 4:19

I met a Korean War veteran the other day, as he sat by a lake fishing. Never a stranger, I struck up a conversation with him. We talked about fishing. He said, "You have to have some patience when you're fishing, as sometimes it takes a while to catch something." As a small boat floated by, I asked him, "Do you catch more fish if you're in the middle of the water or on the edge of the water?" His answer was simple yet profound.

He replied, "It doesn't matter; the fish are gonna bite when they bite. You gotta go where the fish are. You have to go near the water." He looked up from his fishing pole and said, "It's just like if you're gonna catch anyone for the Lord, you gotta go into the world to go get them." Now, you know that's when the real conversation started.

Hey, this morning, I want to remind you that you're near the water. I know you may be on the job, at school, shopping for a new pair of shoes, but if you're a believer, wherever you find yourself, it is a fishing pond. God placed you there to cast your line. How do I do that, you might ask? You cast your line with your attitude, your perseverance, your smile, your patience, and your praise in pain. Check your line. Are you scaring the fish away because your line doesn't look that inviting?

It is not a mistake that you find yourself there today. God placed you there to cast your line and pull someone in when they're ready to bite. The question today is, "What kind of bait are you using?"

TOUCHING STRANGERS
Co-author Carla Barnett

"Now you are no longer strangers to God and foreigners to heaven, but you are members of God's very own family, citizens of God's country, and you belong in God's household with every other Christian."

Ephesians 2:19

R ichard Rinaldi, a New York street photographer, created a fantastic photography series called, "Touching Strangers." He invited total strangers on the street to pose together as a family, capturing a fleeting moment, but the results were terrific. Even though they didn't know each other after posing, the strangers reported having feelings of being connected, having a sense of belonging, and caring for their new family member whom they had just met.

Richard Rinaldi's photo experiment reminds us that we don't live in a selfie kind of world. These strangers were from different backgrounds, genders, and ethnicities, but a simple picture and the thought that this person could be a part of my family touched something deep inside these strangers. It reminded them how connected we are to each other.

What if we thought of each other as family? Listen, I know your co-worker touches a nerve, but what would happen if you envisioned her as your sister or him as your brother? How about that neighbor you avoid speaking to, or the countless strangers you encounter daily? They all have their issues, but guess what? You're not perfect either. We're all connected. Scripture reminds us that we are all made in the image and likeness of God. As believers, our Savior unites us by his precious blood. In other words, in Christ, we have the same DNA.

There are no retakes, cropping, photoshopping, or editing necessary because Jesus took on all the blemishes and imperfections and nailed it to the cross. Imagine God looking at a portrait of His family. What do you suppose He sees? Are you in the picture? Don't allow the enemy to photobomb your picture.

Long ago, Sister Sledge had a song called, "We Are Family." I agree we are a family connected with an everlasting love. You still have a chance to jump in the picture. So smile and strike a pose because salvation is free, and that's a family picture worth more than a thousand words.

THE...EXECUTOR

Jesus said, "For whoever does the will of My Father in heaven is My brother and sister and mother."

Matthew 12:50

Recently, I had some legal documents delivered to me that read, "YOU ARE THE... Executor!" Someone thought enough of me to name me the executor of their will. I'm humbled they had enough faith and trust in me to carry out their last wishes. The executor has one job and one job only: to carry out the desires of the one who left the will. My opinion doesn't matter. What I think doesn't matter. As the executor of the will, I cannot change the will to fit my thoughts of fairness or give possession of an item to someone I believed was a better caretaker. I can't take out parts of the will I don't like. The will stands on its own, and I have to execute it as written.

Well, God thought enough of all of us to name us executors of His will. It's incredibly humbling knowing that God trusts us with such an important task. As executors, we have one job and one job only: execute the will! We don't try to change it. We don't amend it. We don't take out the parts we don't like. God trusts us to open his will every day and read it and follow his instructions. I confess, sometimes, as I read his will, there are objectives in there that are hard to follow, like loving enemies and praying for people who despise you. But, as the executor, my opinion doesn't matter. As the executors, we follow the desires and instructions of the one who left the will. You are the Executor! Now, go out and execute the Lord's will.

THEY'LL GIVE YOU A NAME

"But you are a chosen generation, a royal priesthood, a holy nation, His own special people, that you may proclaim the praises of Him who called you out of darkness into His marvelous light."

1 Peter 2:9

I visit people all day long as a hospital Chaplain. As you can imagine, people are not feeling their best. I minister to people managing terminal illnesses, battling some unknown disease, and others recovering from the trauma of what man has done to man.

136

Regardless of the person, I always introduce myself as the Chaplain and request permission to speak. If invited into the room, we'll discuss the issues that are important to them. The conversations are always interesting, and the Holy Spirit guides those conversations as I try to speak to their needs. It is interesting when the conversation is over and I head toward the door, the names or titles of which I am referred.

The patients usually thank me for the visit, but instead of calling me 'Chaplain,' they'll refer to me by many terms. I've been called 'Father,' 'Reverend,' while a lot call me 'Pastor,' and some even choose to call me by my first name; and then there's my personal favorite, 'Padre.' They are likely responding out of their religious tradition, or perhaps they are responding to the spiritual care I've provided to them.

It reminds me of how God introduces himself in the scripture as Elohim, Jehovah, and Lord, to name just a few. When we spend time with Him, and as He attends to our needs, we respond to Him in the way we came into His presence; and so we sometimes refer to Him by the role He has played for us. We'll call him a Way Maker, a Company Keeper, a Healer, a Lawyer, a Doctor in a sick room, a Miracle Worker because that's who He is in that moment. The question I leave you with today is when people leave your presence, what name do they call you?

REFLECTIONS

ABOUT THE AUTHOR

Photo Credit: Patrick Dean

Tracy Alan Barnett was born and raised in Erie, PA. Tracy was raised in a loving Christian home, by his mother Alice, and received the Lord as his savior at the age of seven. He is a proud graduate of Academy High School in Erie, PA. He joined the United States Air Force immediately following high school and rose through the ranks, and after 26 years of faithful service, retired as a Commissioned Officer.

He began ministry at the age of 19, and his service to the country allowed him to share the gospel with people around the country and many places around the world. For a year, he shared the gospel message in the war-torn country of Afghanistan and saw the power of God's word to sustain and encourage those in battle. Over the years, he has served in various capacities in many churches across the country.

He is now a Board-Certified Chaplain (BCC) specializing in Mental Health issues and serves as a Hospital Chaplain helping veterans recover from the trauma of war. He holds a Master of Divinity from Southwestern Baptist Theological Seminary, and a Master of Human Relations from the University of Oklahoma. He also earned his undergrad in Management from the University of Maryland University College.

Tracy is the author of ***Whispers In The Morning: A Guide to Discovering God's Voice in Your Daily Life***, which was published in 2019 and has blessed hundreds of readers. It is available on Amazon in both print and Kindle formats.

Closing Thoughts

God is intentional and everything that happens in our lives is a part of His plan, but we must open our spiritual ears to hear His voice.

I pray this book has encouraged you to seek God's hand in the small things that happen in your life every day. My deepest desire is that you develop the habit of listening for God's voice in the echoes of your daily life.

If you know of someone who is struggling in one or more of the areas addressed in this book, would you be a blessing and recommend this book as a resource?

If you have any questions or comments, please feel free to reach out to me on Facebook @WhsprMorn, or email: WhsprsMorn@gmail.com.

If this book has been a blessing to you, would you write a few brief sentences as a review on Amazon? This will help others decide if this book is for them. As an author, I value and appreciate your time to write a review.

Looking for more devotions? Follow me on Facebook. I will periodically share new devotions there.